THE PREHISTORIC TEMPLES OF

STONEHENGE & AVEBURY

PHOTOGRAPHS: JOHN GREEN TEXT: R J C ATKINSON

THE PREHISTORIC TEMPLES OF STONEHENGE & AVEBURY

R J C ATKINSON
Professor of Archaeology, University College, Cardiff

Of all the earlier prehistoric monuments of Britain, Avebury and Stonehenge are the most famous. Both are now visited by so many people each year that it has become necessary to fence off parts of them in order to prevent further damage by the feet of too many interested visitors. This booklet describes both of them, with special attention to the illustration of details which can no longer be seen at close range.

STONEHENGE

Stonehenge stands on the southern part of Salisbury Plain, about 8 miles north of Salisbury and 2 miles west of Amesbury. It is the focal point of the densest concentration of Neolithic and Bronze Age monuments anywhere in Britain, and can be regarded as a kind of prehistoric cathedral which endured for 2,000 years.

Like many Christian cathedrals, it has a very long history of building and alteration, which reflects changes in architectural style and fashion, and changes too in the way in which religious beliefs were expressed in tangible form. Excavations have shown that four main periods can be recognized in the building and use of Stonehenge, the third of which can be further divided into

★

LEFT: *Reconstruction (Salisbury Museum) of a Beaker burial near Stonehenge, with pot and bronze knife.*

FACING PAGE: *This aerial view from the south shows the central stones surrounded by the earlier bank and ditch. The white dots within the bank mark the positions of the excavated Aubrey Holes.*

three stages. It is convenient to call these Stonehenge I, II, IIIa, IIIb, IIIc and IV. Various events in this sequence have been dated by the radiocarbon process, which uses specimens of charcoal, bone or antler found in excavations. From these we know that Stonehenge was in use from about 2800 BC until after 1100 BC, a period of more than 17 centuries. This is almost twice as long as the time from the Norman Conquest to the present day.

Stonehenge I consisted of a circular earthwork enclosure about 91m across, surrounded by a bank with a ditch outside it, and a smaller bank outside the ditch, all much flattened by weathering. Originally the main bank was about 1·8m high, and the ditch from which its material was excavated averaged at least 2·1m in depth, though it was dug in an irregular way. This earthwork was constructed in about 2800 BC.

In a broad entrance-gap on the north-east side there stood a pair of stones; and beyond, astride the axis of symmetry, there was a row of four large wooden posts, which perhaps supported timber lintels to form a triple gateway. Nearby to the east there stood a large sarsen stone, probably found in the neighbourhood. During period I this was apparently replaced by the present Heel Stone or Friar's Heel, so called from the legend of an impudent friar who accosted the Devil whilst he was building Stonehenge. The stone thrown by the Devil hit the friar on the heel, but he was unharmed.

The reason for this replacement is unknown. The Heel Stone, larger than the stone which it replaced, now leans towards the centre of the monument, but was originally upright. It weighs about 35 tonnes, and would have needed about 250 men to transport

★

LEFT: *The Heel Stone, seen from the south-east, is now leaning towards the centre of Stonehenge but was originally upright.*

FACING PAGE: *West View of Stonehenge, from* The Ancient History of South Wiltshire, volume II, *by Sir Richard Colt Hoare.*

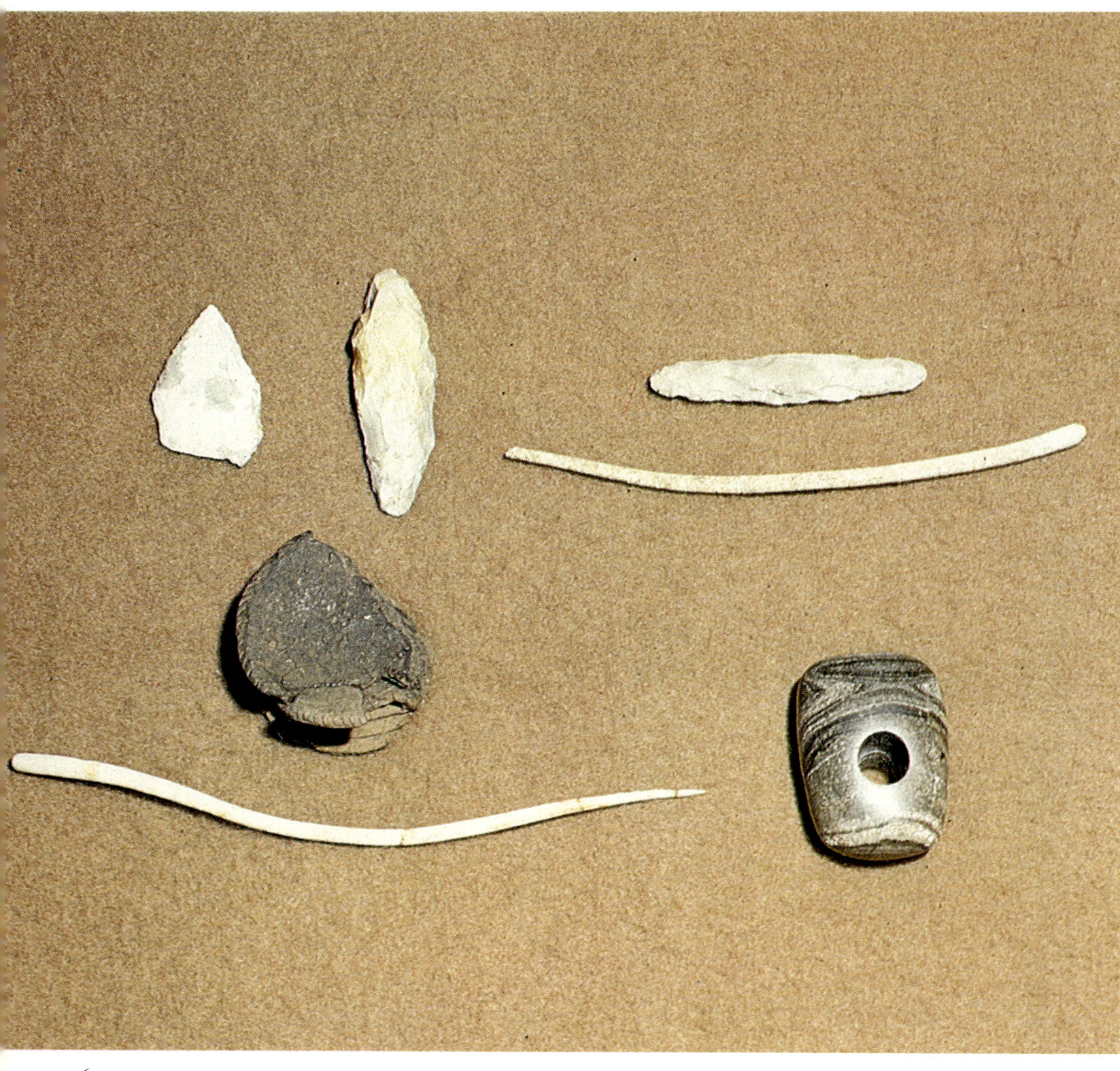

and erect it. If allowance is made for women and children, and for the aged and infirm, the population involved must have been about 500, and must have been drawn from more than the local area. From the start, therefore, Stonehenge seems to have been more than the equivalent of a village church or a parish chapel.

Inside the bank there was a ring of 56 pits, evenly spaced about 4·9m apart; these are now known as the Aubrey Holes after their discoverer, the 17th-century antiquary John Aubrey, who noticed some of them as slight hollows in the turf. About half of them were excavated in the 1920s and are now marked by white concrete discs. They are about 1m wide and deep, with steep sides and flat bottoms. Their purpose is unknown, though it is clear that they never held upright stones or wooden posts, which would have left impressions on the chalk at the bottom. Soon after they were dug they were re-filled with chalk, some of which had been burnt meanwhile. Later they were re-used for burials of cremated human bones, one of which has been dated to about 2200 BC. Some of these burials were accompanied by slender pins of bone and other objects of Late Neolithic type; and there are numerous similar burials inserted into the bank and the silting in the ditch. Other cremation cemeteries of this kind have been found occasionally elsewhere in Britain, in rings of pits and with similar objects.

★

LEFT: *Bone hair-pins, flint implements, a ceremonial mace-head of polished stone, and a broken 'pot-stand' of fired clay, found with cremations in the Aubrey Holes and the bank and ditch.*

FACING PAGE, left: *Sarsen hammers used to shape the stones. The smallest is the size of an orange.*

FACING PAGE, right: *Two of the trilithons, showing the downward taper and curvature of the lintels. In front of them stand two pillars of the bluestone horseshoe. The large fallen stone, paired with the upright on the left, formed the central trilithon. Uniquely, both were dressed smooth on the outer side.*

Stonehenge I seems to have remained in use as a place of neolithic worship and burial for about seven centuries. Then, in period II, it was altered by the addition of the Avenue and the bluestones, about 2100 BC. The Avenue (extended later, in period IV) ran for about 510m from the entrance of the circular earthwork, in a straight line. It was marked out on either side by a bank and ditch, and its mid-line pointed approximately to the sunrise at midsummer. To make the entrance of the earthwork symmetrical to this new axis, it was widened by throwing part of the bank back into the ditch; and the former pair of stones in the entrance, now no longer central, was moved on to the centre line of the nearer part of the Avenue, perhaps to mark the direction of the midsummer sunrise. At the same time the Heel Stone was surrounded by a narrow circular ditch which was almost immediately filled up, possibly as a kind of symbolic protection.

Around the centre the builders of Stonehenge II began to erect a double circle of bluestones, so called from their colour. Microscopical examination of the stones which survive (though re-used in a different way) has shown that they come from the Preseli Mountains in south-west Wales, about 135 miles from Stonehenge. Until recently it was supposed that they were transported directly from there to Stonehenge; but it now seems more

likely that they were first brought to somewhere else on Salisbury Plain, before even Stonehenge I had been built, and that they were later re-used for Stonehenge II. There is no sign of their presence on the site before that period.

These bluestones were set up in two concentric circles about 1·8m apart. On the north-east side there was an entrance marked by extra stones on the inside, which pointed down the Avenue to the midsummer sunrise. On the opposite side a single large hole evidently held a stone of exceptional size, probably the present Altar Stone (p. 14).

Excavations have shown, however, that only a part of this double circle was ever erected. Before the western side was finished, the builders changed their minds and dismantled all the stones already set up. All that now survive are the holes underground in which the stones stood, on either side of the later bluestone circle (p. 15). We know that they were bluestones, because when they were removed small chips of rock were left embedded in the bottoms of the holes, which have been identified microscopically with the existing bluestones.

Probably at this time or slightly earlier the four Station Stones were set up on the line of the Aubrey Holes. Two of them, both of sarsen stone, are still there, one fallen and the other as the battered upright stump of a stone which was formerly higher. The other two have disappeared; but each once stood at the centre of a small ditched enclosure (known rather misleadingly as the North and South Barrows). These are later than the main bank, on which they encroach. The battered Station Stone may be a later replacement of an earlier marker, because it is partly shaped, above

★

LEFT: *The surviving upright of the central trilithon, the tallest stone at Stonehenge, with the tenon on top. The fallen lintel, with mortices, lies in front of it.*

FACING PAGE: *Three uprights of the sarsen circle, showing the upward taper of their shapes.*

and below ground level, in the same way as the sarsen stones of period IIIa (p. 11). The fallen stone, like the Heel Stone, is in its natural state and has not been artificially shaped.

The four Stations lie at the corners of a rectangle, the short sides of which point to the rising sun at midsummer and the setting sun at midwinter, and the long sides to the most southerly rising and most northerly setting of the moon. The latter events occur only once every 18½ years. From period II, therefore, if not before, the users of Stonehenge were concerned to mark in their open-air temple certain significant astronomical directions. This is not to say, however, that they must have worshipped the sun and moon. Most Christian churches, after all, point to the rising sun at the equinoxes.

The builders of Stonehenge II were probably Beaker people, so called from their habit of burying pottery beakers, or drinking-vessels, in graves. Groups of them settled in eastern and southern Britain at various times between 2500 and 2000 BC, and brought with them two practices which gradually transformed the life of the native neolithic population. One was the working of the earliest metals, copper and gold, for tools, weapons and ornaments. The other was the burial of the dead singly under a round barrow instead of communally under a long barrow or in a cremation cemetery. Many of the barrows round Stonehenge are of the Beaker period; and in 1978 a burial of Beaker type was found in the ditch of Stonehenge itself.

The building of Stonehenge II began at a time when the influence of the Beaker people was coming to an end, and they themselves were

*

LEFT: *A former bluestone lintel of period IIIb, with two mortices, re-used as a pillar in the bluestone circle of period IIIc, now fallen.*

FACING PAGE: *Curved lintels of the outer circle, showing a tongued joint.*

gradually mixing with the larger native population to produce new and vigorous societies. In just the same way the Norman invaders of England, relatively few in number, had a profound effect on the way of life of the English of the Middle Ages. In Wessex we can see the rise in the Early Bronze Age, between 2000 and 1500 BC, of a number of rich and powerful dynasties of chiefs, whose wealth came mainly from large flocks and herds, but may have derived in part also from their control over the growing trade in bronze tools and weapons, manufactured for markets on the continent. Many of these chiefs and their families lie buried around Stonehenge in cemeteries of round barrows.

These people were the builders of Stonehenge III, the most remarkable stone circle in Europe. In the British Isles there are altogether about 900 stone circles, and a few more in Brittany. Some of them, such as those at Avebury, are considerably larger than Stonehenge; but none rivals it in the height of its stones, the precision of their plan or the refinements of their shaping and jointing. None but Stonehenge, moreover, had stone lintels on top of the uprights. In all these respects it is unique, and represents the culmination of a very long tradition of building with large stones.

The first stage of this great monument, Stonehenge IIIa, consisted of an outer circle of 30 uprights of uniform height, capped by a horizontal ring of stone lintels. This enclosed symmetrically a horseshoe of five trilithons (so called from the Greek for 'three stones'), each of a pair of uprights supporting a lintel, rising in height towards the central trilithon. All these stones are of sarsen, like the stones of Avebury. Like them too they were transported from the Marlborough Downs, some 20 miles to the north. Both circle and horseshoe have been laid out with great accuracy, in spite of the enormous mass of the stones, of which the heaviest weighs about 50 tonnes.

Analysis of the plan of these stones shows that the builders may have used the 'megalithic yard' (p.26) and a 'megalithic rod' of $2\frac{1}{2}$ megalithic yards, or 2·073m. The outer ring of uprights fits very well

between two concentric circles with circumferences of 45 and 48 rods; and each upright is close to one rod wide, half-a-rod thick and half-a-rod from its neighbours. The outer four trilithons are an equally good fit to an ellipse with major and minor diameters of 27 and 17 megalithic yards, and a perimeter of 28 rods. This is one of the most striking pieces of evidence for the possible use of these hypothetical prehistoric units.

All these stones have had their surfaces shaped and smoothed by pounding them with stone mauls or hammers, as big as a football. The stone is so hard that it will blunt the cutting edge of a bronze chisel almost at once, so that hammering was the only way of working it. This must have been done before the stones were erected, when they were still lying on the ground and could be turned over with levers. To shape them in this way needed enormous labour, because a man could probably dress only about 0·14 square metres in a working day, or less if the natural surface was very rough. Many of the worn and discarded hammers were later re-used as packing-stones round the bases of the uprights, to hold them tight in their stone-holes.

The shapes of the stones show subtle refinements. The uprights taper towards the top with a slightly convex outline, perhaps to give an illusion of increased height. The lintels are not rectangular blocks, but are cut to curves; and the trilithon lintels are wider above than below, so that their sides incline towards the ground, which has the effect of making them look vertical. These are all architectural devices used deliberately only at a much later date, in the marble temples of the classical world, like the Parthenon. It is possible,

★

LEFT: *Carvings of a bronze dagger and axe-heads on the inner side of a trilithon.*

FACING PAGE: *This grooved bluestone in the horseshoe of period IIIc was formerly jointed to another, with a corresponding ridge, to form a composite stone matching the Altar Stone in width in period IIIb.*

though we cannot be sure, that the builders of Stonehenge were seeking, more crudely and with much more intractable material, to achieve the same architectural effects.

In addition, the sarsen stones are jointed together. Hollow mortice holes on the undersides of the lintels fit over tenons projecting from the tops of the uprights; and the lintels of the outer circle are interlocked by vertical tongues and grooves. These are carpenters' joints, not masons', imitated from an earlier tradition of working in timber.

This unique construction was completed by a pair of large sarsen stones, about 5·5m high, standing close together in the entrance of the earthwork, so as to frame between them the sun rising over the horizon at midsummer for an observer at the centre. One of them has disappeared. The other, long since fallen, is known as the Slaughter Stone, a name invented by over-imaginative antiquaries for whom it conjured up visions of bloody Druidical sacrifices.

The building of Stonehenge IIIa began about 2000 BC and probably took many years to complete. The most difficult operations in transporting and raising the stones would have needed about 1500 able-bodied men, representing a total population two or three times as large. Though we cannot estimate the size of prehistoric communities with any confidence, it is unlikely that the local region of Salisbury Plain could have provided all the labour required. Almost certainly this undertaking needed the co-operation of tribes or clans spread over a much wider area; and this implies some kind of central and wide-ranging authority, though its nature remains tantalisingly obscure.

The subsequent alterations concern the bluestones, already used in Stonehenge II and then dismantled. In their present form they are the remains, much ruined, of a circle of about 60 stones inside the sarsen circle, and a horseshoe of 19 stones inside the horseshoe of sarsen trilithons. This is their final arrangement in period IIIc; but it contains some re-used components of an earlier bluestone structure, all of which have been shaped

and some of which were jointed together. In the present circle, all but two of the surviving stones are natural slabs or pillars which have not been artificially shaped. The two exceptions are lintels re-used on end as pillars, with their mortice holes facing outwards so as not to be seen from the centre. Both have since fallen over.

In the present bluestone horseshoe there are three pillars which show the remains of projecting tenons on their tops. These have been deliberately battered down with stone hammers; but enough survives to show that they were once there. In addition, one very long pillar has a deep groove worked all the way down one side, which is matched by a corresponding ridge on another, now only a buried stump. These two must formerly have been jointed, perhaps to provide a composite stone of about the same width and length as those of the Altar Stone, the largest of all the surviving bluestones. Clearly all these jointed stones belonged to some former structure, which must have included at least two bluestone trilithons.

Excavations have revealed some of the holes in which these shaped bluestones stood. They follow the line of the later bluestone horseshoe, and close its open end to form an ellipse, inside which there were extra holes for stones which seem to have marked the direction of midsummer sunrise. The

★

LEFT: *The central pillar of the bluestone horseshoe of period IIIc, now fallen, with traces of a battered-down tenon on the near end.*

FACING PAGE: *Carvings, full size, of Early Bronze Age axe-heads on the outer face of stone 4 of the sarsen circle (the stones are numbered clockwise from the entrance).*

FOLLOWING PAGE, left: *This is the best preserved part of the sarsen circle. The entrance was beneath the middle of the three lintels.*

FOLLOWING PAGE, right: *Part of the outer circle of sarsens, spanning the entrance, with stones of the bluestone circle inside it.*

spacing of the holes discovered suggests that only about 20 of the bluestones were used in this elliptical setting of period IIIb.

We know that in the final re-arrangement about 80 stones were used, so that about 60 remain to be accounted for. It seems to have been the builders' intention to erect these in the two rings of Y and Z holes, discovered in excavations outside the sarsen circle; but it is clear that this project, like the building of the double circle of Stonehenge II, was never completed. On the east side several of the Y and Z holes are irregularly spaced and only partially excavated; and in the Z ring one hole was never dug at all. None of these holes contains the impression of a stone on its bottom. Evidently this idea was abandoned before any of the remaining bluestones of period IIIb had been erected.

At this point, which can be dated about 1550 BC, close to the end of the Early Bronze Age, the ellipse of dressed and jointed bluestones around the centre was dismantled, and all the bluestones were re-arranged in the circle and horseshoe whose remains we can see today. The Y and Z holes were left open, and filled up slowly with soil blown by the wind from cultivated fields near by. This final reconstruction brought to an end the long building history of Stonehenge.

How long thereafter it continued as a place of worship we cannot be sure; but it must have been for at least 500 years. In period IV, about 1100 BC, the Avenue was extended from the end of the first straight stretch built in period II to the River Avon near West Amesbury. This must mean that Stonehenge, to which the Avenue leads, was still in use at that date, and afterwards.

The later history of Stonehenge is one of ruin and decay. Many of its stones are now missing, probably because they were broken up for building stone in the Middle Ages, perhaps after being deliberately pulled down. They were a convenient source of stone, because the nearest workable quarry is 13 miles away. It is even possible that in Roman times some of the stones were broken up and scattered in fragments, to discourage nationalist sentiments

Continued on page 18

amongst the conquered British population. Since 1958 a number of fallen and leaning stones have been re-erected and straightened, so as to restore the monument to its state at the end of the 18th century AD.

We shall never know what religious beliefs Stonehenge represents, or what forms of worship or ceremonies took place within it. These are questions, like many others about the prehistoric past, for which the evidence provides no real answers, either because it is not there, or because it is completely ambiguous.

Some of the sarsen stones bear the weathered remains of carvings of a bronze dagger and of numerous bronze axe-heads, discovered in 1953; but we do not know whether these are religious symbols, or votive offerings, or something else. On one of the trilithons there is a squarish outline, resembling carvings in neolithic tombs in Brittany which are thought to be much simplified representations of a mother-goddess; but this too leads only to speculation. There can be no certainty.

In recent years many suggestions have been made about the possible use of Stonehenge as an astronomical observatory, to record the movements of the rising and setting sun and moon along the horizon, and to predict eclipses. All that we can be certain of is that from period II onwards the axis of symmetry does seem to point roughly to the midsummer sunrise, and that the Station Stones could indicate extreme positions of the moon on the horizon. Beyond this there can be no certainty, because the monument is now so ruined that it is impossible to be sure what sight-lines may have once been built into its structure.

⋆

LEFT: *Carving, perhaps a symbol for a 'Mother-goddess', on the inside of the fourth trilithon.*

FACING PAGE: *The view along the astronomical axis of Stonehenge, towards the point of midsummer sunrise.*

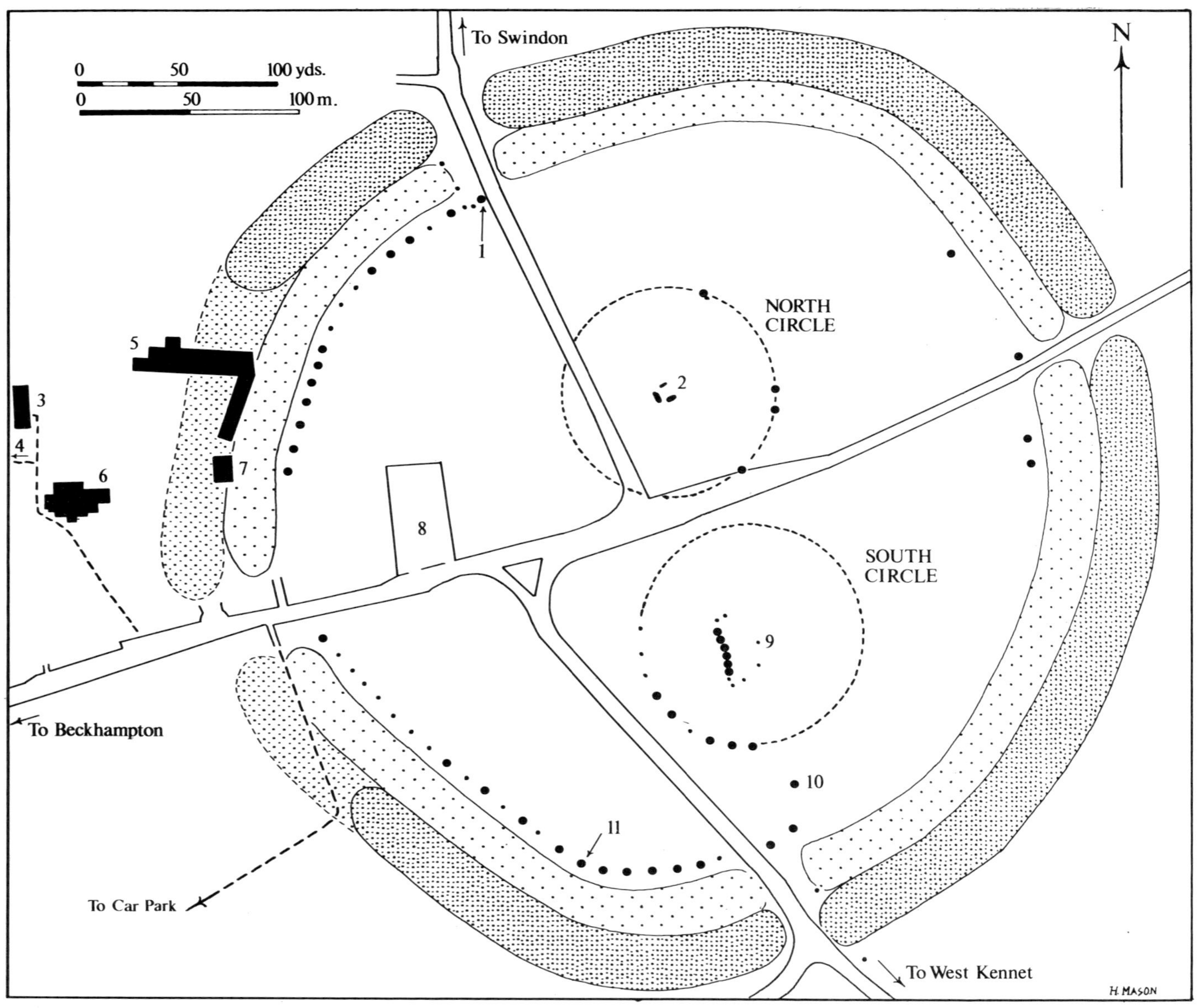

Avebury

1 The Swindon Stone

2 The Cove

3 The Alexander Keiller Museum

4 Avebury Manor

5 The Old Barn and Folk Life Museum

6 Avebury Church

7 The National Trust Shop

8 Car Park

9 The Obelisk

10 The Ring Stone

11 The Barber Stone

Bank

Ditch

Former bank

FACING PAGE: *Here Avebury is seen in a bird's-eye view from the south-west. The roads still pass through the entrances of the prehistoric earthwork which surrounds part of the village.*

AVEBURY

The great earthwork and stone circles of Avebury lie in an undulating landscape which forms a westwards extension of the high chalk downs of North Wiltshire, 5 miles west of Marlborough and 1 mile north of the Bath Road (A4). With one exception, it is the largest of all the open-air temples of prehistoric Britain.

It is indeed so large that it now encloses part of the village of Avebury, whose houses and roads obscure its original plan. To understand what Avebury was like in prehistoric times, the visitor must take a walk of about 1100m. Starting in the car-park in the village, the route runs left-handed around the Red Lion Inn to the north entrance of the circle; thence round the western half to the south entrance; and from there northwards again to the car-park.

Prehistoric Avebury is enclosed by an enormous earthwork, a ditch with a bank outside it. The area inside the ditch is about 10 hectares. Just within the ditch are the remains of a circle of standing stones, originally about 100 in number, the largest circle of its kind in Europe. In the interior, parts of two smaller circles survive, each with other settings of stones inside them. From the south and west entrances avenues of standing stones ran formerly for distances of over 1½ miles.

These features are described below in detail. Meanwhile, however, the visitor must understand that most of the prehistoric stones of Avebury, of which there were at least 180 within the earthwork and perhaps 400 more in the two avenues outside, have been pulled down and buried, or broken up for building material, during the last thousand years. All but a few of those now standing were discovered

★

LEFT: *The nearest stone, called the Barber Stone, now set upright, killed an itinerant barber-surgeon who was helping to overthrow it early in the 14th century* AD.

FACING PAGE: *The north-west quarter of Avebury, from the north entrance.*

and re-erected in the 1930s. This work was done by Alexander Keiller (assisted by Stuart Piggott), who purchased the Avebury monument in 1934 and from whom it was subsequently acquired by its present owners, the National Trust. The positions of stones which had been broken up were marked with low pyramids of concrete.

Up to the Norman Conquest, probably, most of the original stones remained intact, though some must have fallen and others may have been broken up to provide material for the Saxon church and village of Avebury. By the 14th century, however, it is clear that stones were being deliberately pulled down and buried, possibly at fairly regular intervals, so that the Church could demonstrate to each succeeding generation of inhabitants its abhorrence of pagan practices which may still have survived from an earlier time.

Dramatic evidence for one of these possibly ceremonial fellings comes from a stone in the south-west quadrant, now known as the Barber Stone. When this was pulled over and buried, it crushed to death a man whose leather wallet contained the scissors and probe of an itinerant barber-surgeon, and coins dated soon after AD 1300.

Later, from the 17th century onwards, stones were destroyed or buried in increasing numbers, for building material or to clear the ground for ploughing. The 18th-century antiquary William Stukeley described and illustrated how the stones were felled over a pit filled with burning straw and faggots, cooled locally with streams of cold water to set up thermal stresses, and then shattered to fragments with blows from a sledgehammer. Some of the innumerable blocks of stone in the walls of Avebury are still reddened by fire; and one stone, just south of the village street at the west entrance, has been partly reconstructed from its broken fragments.

The earthwork

The great earthwork is one of the largest enclosures of early prehistoric Britain, with a circumference along the crest of the bank of about 1350m. Though it is impressive even today, it has been severely eroded and silted up during the last 45 centuries. Originally the ditch was more than 9m deep, with sides much steeper than today, plunging to a flat bottom about 4m wide. At the top it was narrower than it is now, because its width has been increased by long erosion.

The 150,000 tonnes of chalk rubble laboriously excavated from the ditch, with pick-axes made from the antlers of red deer, were hauled or carried to the surface in wicker baskets and piled up outside to form a rather irregular rampart, the centre-line of which had probably been marked out in advance by a smaller bank, only a metre or so high. In places the inner edge of this great bank was contained by a wall of rough chalk blocks; but this was a device adopted only by the tidier gangs of builders, and was not a constant architectural feature around the whole circuit of the bank.

When it was finished, the average height of the bank would have been about 6·4m and its inner edge would have been separated from the ditch by a broad flat platform or terrace. Traces of this can still be seen to the east of the south entrance. At this entrance, and presumably at the others, the butt-end of the ditch was neatly squared off at right-angles.

Of the four entrance-gaps through the earthwork, those to the north, south and west are known from excavations to be original. The east entrance, through which the old road from London to Bath used to pass, has not been tested by excavation, but is probably an original feature as well.

The great stone circle

About 12m inside the inner edge of the original ditch the builders erected a ring of large sarsen stones. There were probably about 100 of these, and they formed the largest prehistoric stone circle in Europe. They must have been dragged on sledges and rollers from the high chalk downs a mile or two to the east, where similar slabs and boulders still lie thickly on the surface, the remains of a thin layer of hard sandstone which was laid down in geological times over the surface of the chalk.

The surviving stones of this circle vary in size, and it is clear that no effort was made to achieve a uniform height. On the average their weight is about 15 tonnes, but individual stones depart widely from this figure. The heaviest ones weigh three times as much.

This ring of stones evidently had four entrances, corresponding roughly but not exactly to the four

★

LEFT: *A stone just south of the west entrance, reconstructed from its broken fragments.*

FACING PAGE: *The bank and ditch, looking east from the south entrance. Originally the bank was separated from the deep narrow ditch by a broad platform, and its inner edge was retained in places by a low wall of chalk blocks.*

entrances of the surrounding earthwork. Each was flanked by a pair of stones of exceptional size. At the south both survive; at the north one is still standing (the so-called Swindon Stone) and William Stukeley records that the other, now destroyed, was even larger. At the east entrance a large fallen stone just north of the trackway must be the survivor of a similar pair.

As the plan (p. 20) shows, this great ring of stones, where it has been excavated and restored around the west side of Avebury, did not follow the circumference of a true circle. This may be simply the result of the difficulty of setting out on the ground a true circle with a diameter of about 335m with no more than a centre peg and a graduated measuring-cord. Another possibility is that the surrounding earthwork was built first, and that the great stone ring was erected so as to run parallel to the inner edge of the ditch, itself irregular in plan. It has been suggested, however, that the stone ring conforms to an elaborate and complex geometrical construction, based on a unit of measurement (the 'megalithic yard' of 0·829m) whose use has been inferred from many other smaller stone circles in Britain. Pending further excavations in the eastern half of Avebury, it is not possible to make any sensible choice between these explanations.

This great circle of standing stones enclosed two smaller circles of about the same size, and presumably of the same origin.

The North Circle

Only four stones of this circle now survive, two upright and two fallen. Their positions and spacing, with another stone recorded by Stukeley in 1723–24, suggest that originally it contained 27 stones, with a

★

LEFT: *The south-west quarter, seen from the south entrance.*

FACING PAGE: *The view from the South Circle to the south entrance.*

diameter of about 97·5m. Stukeley also recorded three stones of an inner circle with a diameter of about 42·7m and an original number of 12. Of this nothing now remains above ground; but a pipe trench cut in 1964 revealed a burning-pit, used to destroy a stone, on the line of this inner circle.

At the centre of the North Circle, to the east of the Swindon road and north-east of the Red Lion Inn, two very large stones still stand at right angles and a third, to the north-west, was recorded by Stukeley as having existed in the memory of his informants in the village. These evidently formed a kind of huge unroofed sentry-box, open to the north-east, as the focal point of the North Circle and presumably as its central shrine. Similar constructions are known from three other prehistoric sites in Britain, but the function of all of them is unknown. Stukeley called this 'The Cove'.

★

LEFT: *The two surviving stones of the Cove, at the centre of the North Circle, with one of the latter's stones beyond, seen from the west.*

ABOVE: *The 'Swindon Stone', at the west of the north entrance.*

FACING PAGE: *The surviving arc of the Southern Circle, with the entrance of the Great Circle beyond to the south.*

The South Circle

The western half of this circle was excavated and restored in 1939. It seems to have consisted originally of 29 stones lying on a circle about 103·6m in diameter. At the centre there was a single taller stone, already fallen in Stukeley's day, which he called the Obelisk. It has since disappeared, but its site is marked by a concrete pyramid of larger size. No evidence was found for an inner circle.

To the west of the Obelisk the excavators found a row of nine smaller buried stones and stone-holes, with an extra hole to the east at either end; and outside the circle to the south they uncovered the stump of a stone called by Stukeley the Ring Stone, because it was perforated by a natural hole. These latter stones were all packed round their bases with chalk blocks from the lowest levels of the ditch, showing that they were put up after the earthwork had been built.

The Avenues

The south entrance of Avebury was formerly connected to the concentric stone circles on Overton Hill, called the Sanctuary by Stukeley, by an avenue of two parallel lines of standing stones. The Sanctuary was recorded in 1723 and destroyed in the following year; but its site was identified and excavated in 1930.

The northern part of this avenue was excavated and restored by Keiller and Piggott in 1934–35 and 1939. It appears at first sight to follow a sinuous course, but accurate survey suggests that it is made up of a series of straight stretches, with a fairly uniform width of about 28·4m. The stones are

★

LEFT: *The row of smaller stones (called the Z Stones), west of the Obelisk in the South Circle, looking south.*

FACING PAGE: *The restored part of the West Kennet Avenue, looking north towards Avebury over the skyline. This shows that the Avenue changes direction along its course.*

spaced along its length at intervals of about 15m apart, with two contrasting shapes alternating lengthwise and transversely—a parallel-sided pillar and a broader diamond or lozenge shape, standing on one point. The suggestion that these are male and female symbols is plausible but incapable of proof. Two burials associated with these stones show that they were erected in the Beaker period, between 2500 and 2000 BC.

Beyond the restored part only a very few stones survive; but the continuation of this West Kennet Avenue (which passes through the village of that name) right up to the Sanctuary has been confirmed by excavation. Its total length is about 1½ miles.

In his book on Avebury, published in 1743, Stukeley claimed that a similar avenue ran from the west entrance south-westwards to and beyond the hamlet of Beckhampton. Until recently it has been supposed that this was a product of his too-vivid imagination. In 1968, however, cable-trenches in Avebury village and along the Bath Road at Beckhampton simultaneously provided evidence for the former existence of standing stones on Stukeley's suggested line. His Beckhampton Avenue has thus now to be taken seriously, though further confirmatory evidence is needed. It may be that the two enigmatic standing stones a short way north of Beckhampton (known as the Longstones or Adam and Eve) formed part of it.

The date and purpose of Avebury

There is no direct evidence for the date at which any part of Avebury was built, nor do we know whether the earthwork and the stone circles and avenues were planned and executed as a single project, or whether they can be divided into separate and successive phases of construction. The finds from the excavations (which can be seen in the Alexander Keiller Museum beyond the church) suggest a date or dates in the range 2500–2000 BC. This is in the Late Neolithic period, when the Beaker people were already colonising Britain from the Continent. We know from radiocarbon dates that three other open-air embanked sanctuaries of

similarly exceptional size were built elsewhere in Wiltshire and Dorset during this same period.

The purpose of Avebury is equally unknown in detail. It is reasonable to assume that amongst other things, perhaps, it was a temple or a place of worship; but the evidence gives us no hints of what was worshipped, or how. All we can say is that for its builders it must have been of exceptional importance, because of the enormous labour which was devoted to the construction of its surrounding earthwork and to the transport and erection of its stones.

Neither Avebury nor Stonehenge is typical of the prehistoric temples of Britain. The stone circles and earthwork of Avebury are exceptionally large, and the architectural refinements of Stonehenge are without parallel. Both of them show, however, that 4,000 years ago our prehistoric ancestors were capable of feats of design and practical engineering which can stand comparison, given the changed circumstances, with those of today. They laid the foundations on which we now build.

Finds from excavations at Stonehenge are displayed in the Salisbury Museum, and those from Avebury in the Alexander Keiller Museum behind the church in the village.

*

LEFT: *The Longstones, or Adam and Eve, near Beckhampton. The nearer stone was perhaps part of Stukeley's Beckhampton Avenue, and the further part of a circle or 'cove'.*

BACK COVER: *The east side of Stonehenge, showing the greater height of the trilithons* (left) *and the curvature of their lintels.*

ACKNOWLEDGMENTS

The publishers are grateful for assistance from the Devizes and Salisbury Museums and the Department of the Environment. The photographs are by John Green, except pp 3, 21, Aerofilms Ltd; p 5, John Freeman, reproduced by courtesy of the Society of Antiquaries; those on pp 2, 6, 8, are by courtesy of the Salisbury Museum. The line drawings on the inside front cover and p 20 are by H. Mason.

SBN 85372 305 2